W9-BCO-961

VON MILLER

BY JOE L. MORGAN

GRIDIRON GREATS
PRO FOOTBALL'S BEST PLAYERS

AARON RODGERS

ANTONIO BROWN

DREW BREES

J.J. WATT

JULIO JONES

ROB GRONKOWSKI

RUSSELL WILSON

TOM BRADY

VON MILLER

GRIDIRON GREATS
PRO FOOTBALL'S BEST PLAYERS

VON MILLER

BY JOE L. MORGAN

MASON CREST

Mason Crest
450 Parkway Drive, Suite D
Broomall, Pennsylvania 19008
(866) MCP-BOOK (toll-free)
www.masoncrest.com

First printing
9 8 7 6 5 4 3 2 1

ISBN (hardback) 978-1-4222-4076-2
ISBN (series) 978-1-4222-4067-0
ISBN (ebook) 978-1-4222-7727-0

Library of Congress Cataloging-in-Publication Data

Names: Morgan, Joe L., author.
Title: Von Miller / Joe L. Morgan.
Description: Broomall, Pennsylvania : Mason Crest, an imprint of National
  Highlights, Inc., [2018] | Series: Gridiron greats: Pro football's best
  players.
Identifiers: LCCN 2018020764 (print) | LCCN 2018024710 (ebook) | ISBN
  9781422277270 (eBook) | ISBN 9781422240762 (hardback) | ISBN 9781422240670
  (series)
Subjects: LCSH: Miller, Von, 1989—Juvenile literature. | Linebackers
  (Football)—United States—Biography—Juvenile literature. | Football
  players—United States—Biography—Juvenile literature.
Classification: LCC GV939.M52 (ebook) | LCC GV939.M52 M67 2018 (print) | DDC
  796.332092 [B]—dc23
LC record available at https://lccn.loc.gov/2018020764

Developed and Produced by National Highlights Inc.
Editor: Andrew Luke
Interior and cover design: Jana Rade, impact studios
Production: Michelle Luke

QR CODES AND LINKS TO THIRD-PARTY CONTENT

CONTENTS

KEY ICONS TO LOOK FOR:

Words to Understand: These words with their easy-to-understand definitions will increase the reader's understanding of the text while building vocabulary skills.

Sidebars: This boxed material within the main text allows readers to build knowledge, gain insights, explore possibilities, and broaden their perspectives by weaving together additional information to provide realistic and holistic perspectives.

Educational Videos: Readers can view videos by scanning our QR codes, providing them with additional educational content to supplement the text. Examples include news coverage, moments in history, speeches, iconic sports moments and much more!

Text-Dependent Questions: These questions send the reader back to the text for more careful attention to the evidence presented there.

Research Projects: Readers are pointed toward areas of further inquiry connected to each chapter. Suggestions are provided for projects that encourage deeper research and analysis.

Series Glossary of Key Terms: This back-of-the book glossary contains terminology used throughout this series. Words found here increase the reader's ability to read and comprehend higher-level books and articles in this field.

WORDS TO UNDERSTAND

ASTHMA – a chronic lung disorder that is marked by recurring episodes of airway obstruction (as from bronchospasm) manifested by labored breathing accompanied especially by wheezing and coughing and by a sense of constriction in the chest, and that is triggered by hyper reactivity to various stimuli (such as allergens or rapid change in air temperature)

LINEBACKER – a position on the defensive unit of a football team just behind the defensive line and in front of the defensive backfield

RESPECTIVE – belonging or relating to each one of the people or things that have been mentioned

SIGNATURE – something (such as a tune, style, or logo) that serves to set apart or identify

STEREOTYPE – to believe unfairly that all people or things with a particular characteristic are the same

TOUTED – made much of; promoted; talked up

CHAPTER 1

GREATEST MOMENTS

VON MILLER'S NFL CAREER

Von Miller does not instantly evoke a **stereotypical** defensive player. He wears large, thick-rimmed black eyeglasses, sort of as a **signature**. He is also soft spoken and humble; but at almost 6 feet 3 inches (1.9 m) and 246 lbs (112 kg), the former 2nd overall pick of the 2011 NFL Draft has been a beast on the football field. Born March 26, 1989, in Dallas, TX, to former high school athletes and the owners of a power supply company (Power Guardian Inc.)—Von Miller Sr. and Gloria Miller—Von Miller Jr. overcame poor vision and **asthma** as a child to become one of the NFL's elite pass rushers.

Miller was a highly **touted** defensive player coming out of college. The Denver Broncos chose him with a high selection in the draft, a draft that saw many other future great players enter the league such as Cam Newton (number 1 overall pick and future NFL MVP), wide receivers A.J. Green and Julio Jones (drafted **respectively** 4th and 6th), J.J. Watt from Wisconsin with the 11th pick overall, and a diamond in the rough who has evolved into one of the best cornerbacks in the game, Richard Sherman (selected in the 5th round of the 2011 draft with the 154th overall pick).

VON MILLER'S CAREER HIGHLIGHTS

Miller, for his time in the NFL through 2017, has accomplished these career highlights:

- Named to the NFL All-Rookie team (2011)
- Named AP NFL Defensive Rookie of the Year (2011)
- Named Super Bowl MVP (Super Bowl 50)
- Named to NFL Pro Bowl five times (2011, 2012, 2014, 2015, 2016)
- Finished in the top ten for the season in sacks five times (2011, 2012, 2014, 2015, 2016)

MILLER'S GREATEST CAREER MOMENTS

It can be difficult to fully appreciate how great Miller is not only at the **linebacker** position, but as a defender. His presence on the field changes how plays are run and the type of blocking needed by the offensive line to protect a quarterback or help a running play be successful. Miller's accomplishments are on the level of some of the greatest in the game.

An article posted on NFL.com by columnist Adam Shein on June 9, 2017, listed Miller as the second-best defensive player in the NFL, behind defensive end Khalil Mack (Oakland Raiders), and ahead of linebacker Luke Kuechly of the Carolina Panthers at number three (a three-time Butkus award winner, twice in the NFL and once in college), and defensive end J.J. Watt (Houston Texans), who was ranked as the sixth-best defender in the NFL.

VON MILLER'S GREATEST CAREER MOMENTS

HERE IS A LIST OF SOME OF THE GREATEST MOMENTS ACHIEVED BY VON MILLER DURING HIS TIME IN THE NFL SO FAR.

FIRST NFL SACK

Miller wasted no time establishing himself as a force to be dealt with as a defender. In his second NFL game Miller faced an Andy Dalton-led Cincinnati Bengals. Little did Dalton know that he would become Miller's first career sack victim.

Von Miller overwhelms his blocker to bring down Cincinnati Bengals QB Andy Dalton, September 18, 2011, for his first career NFL sack.

MILLER SETS BRONCOS PLAYOFF SACK RECORD

Miller established the sack record for the Denver Broncos with a 2.5-sack performance in the AFC Championship Game against the New England Patriots on January 24, 2016. For the game Miller had 4 tackles and an interception (see number five below).

Broncos DE DeMarcus Ware (58) and Miller team up in this second-quarter play to sack QB Tom Brady, giving each a half a sack in a 2016 AFC Championship game matchup on January 24, 2016.

FIRST INTERCEPTION FOR A TOUCHDOWN

In a game against Tampa Bay Buccaneers on December 2, 2012, Miller picked off a pass thrown by Tampa Bay quarterback Josh Freeman with four minutes left in the 3rd quarter to make the score 27–10. The interception and return was Miller's first scoring play in the NFL and helped the Broncos clinch a playoff spot and division title.

Miller is in perfect position to pick off a Tampa Bay Buccaneers QB Josh Freeman pass on a 3rd-quarter play for 6 points in a December 2, 2012, game.

FIRST FUMBLE RECOVERY FOR A TOUCHDOWN

Having already experienced the thrill of scoring a touchdown in the 2012 season, Miller found another opportunity in a game against the New England Patriots on November 24, 2013. Miller produced the first score of the game in the 1st quarter, scooping up a fumble that he carried 60 yards for a touchdown.

Miller scrambles 60 yards on fumble recovery for a touchdown in a November 24, 2013, game against the New England Patriots.

FIRST PLAYOFF INTERCEPTION

In a game against the New England Patriots on January 24, 2016, Miller not only sacked Patriots QB Tom Brady 2.5 times, he also picked off a Brady pass, the first time he intercepted a pass in the playoffs. Miller's play in that game positioned the Broncos well for their next challenge, which would be against the NFC Champion Carolina Panthers in Super Bowl 50.

Miller drops back into coverage against New England TE Rob Gronkowski in a 2nd-quarter play that saw him come up with his first playoff interception as a pro.

SUPER BOWL 50 MVP

2015 was a magical season for Miller. He recorded 30 tackles and 11 sacks for the season, helping to lead the Broncos to 12 wins and 4 losses. In the AFC Championship playoff game on January 24, 2016, against the New England Patriots, Miller sacked QB Tom Brady 2.5 times and intercepted a pass on the way to a 20–18 victory and a berth in Super Bowl 50. Miller's efforts in the Super Bowl against the 1-loss Carolina Panthers included 2 forced fumbles (one that led to a touchdown), 2.5 sacks, and 5 tackles. His effort earned the Broncos a victory and Miller MVP honors.

Miller's fantastic play in Super Bowl 50 against the Carolina Panthers results in his first Super Bowl MVP honor.

THIRD FASTEST TO 50 NFL CAREER SACKS

Miller became the third-fastest player in NFL history to record 50 sacks in his career. Behind only Reggie White (40 games) and Derrick Thomas (54 games), Miller recorded his 50th sack in a September 17, 2015, game (his 58th) against the Kansas City Chiefs

Miller shows his sack dance moves after bringing Kansas City Chiefs QB Alex Smith down in a September 17, 2015, division rivalry game.

FIRST SEASON WITH 10 OR MORE SACKS

Miller, the 2nd overall pick in the 2011 NFL Draft, had great expectations on his shoulders coming from College Station (Texas A&M University). He did not disappoint. Miller recorded 11.5 sacks in his first complete season with the Broncos, earning NFL All-Rookie team honors and setting him on a pace that through 2017 places him number two on the Broncos all-time sack list (behind linebacker Simon Fletcher, who played for the Broncos 1985–1995).

Highlight video of Miller's 2011 rookie season and some of the 11.5 sacks that he recorded.

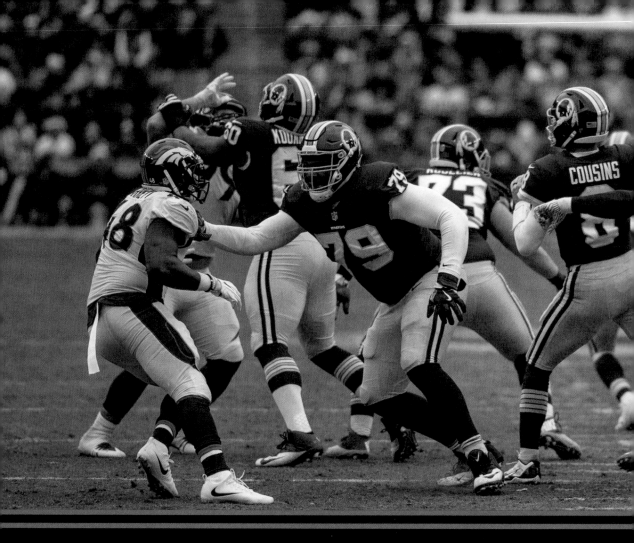

TEXT-DEPENDENT QUESTIONS:

1. How many sacks did Von Miller have for his rookie season in 2011? Where does Von Miller rank on Denver's all-time career sack list?

2. What quarterback did Von Miller sack for his 50th career sack? What team was the sack recorded against? In what season did this sack occur?

3. How many sacks did Von Miller have in Super Bowl 50 against the Carolina Panthers? How many fumbles did Miller force in the game?

Miller is considered to be one of the best pass rushers and overall defenders in the NFL.

RESEARCH PROJECT:

Von Miller was named the NFL's Defensive Rookie of the Year for his play in 2011. He followed up this honor by becoming the MVP of Super Bowl 50 in 2016, as his Denver Broncos topped the Carolina Panthers 24–10, February 7, 2016. Doing a little research, how many players over the last twenty years (since 1998) were either named Rookie of the Year (Defensive or Offensive), Most Valuable Player (Defensive or Offensive) or Super Bowl MVP?

WORDS TO UNDERSTAND

CAMPAIGN – a connected series of operations designed to bring about a particular result

ENTREPRENEUR – one who organizes, manages, and assumes the risks of a business or enterprise

PERSEVERE – to continue doing something or trying to do something even though it is difficult

STRIVE – to try very hard to do or achieve something

CHAPTER 2

THE ROAD TO THE TOP

Von Miller tells a story about how when he was younger, his mother would take him to football practices with his breathing machine in the car because he suffered from asthma as a child. This enabled him to take precautions concerning his condition in between defensive and offensive plays. This commitment and devotion on the part of his mother and parents also taught Miller important life lessons, such as how to **persevere** and continue to **strive**, even when dealing with a situation that may be difficult to handle.

Miller grew up in a home that was **entrepreneurial** in nature. His parents, Von Sr. and Gloria, own and operate a power supply company. The company, which is based in DeSoto, TX, provides supplies throughout southwest Texas, and as far north as Denver, CO, (where Miller now plays football). Miller also grew up with a younger brother named Vince.

ATHLETIC ACCOMPLISHMENTS IN HIGH SCHOOL AND COLLEGE

From early on, it seemed that football was something that Miller was going to pursue as a career. Having an athletic family (both of Von's parents played sports in high school) and weighing more than 200 lbs at 6 feet 3 inches (1.9 m) meant that Miller had the build to excel in many different types of sports before ultimately determining that he was going to focus on football.

HIGH SCHOOL

Miller entered DeSoto High School in his hometown of DeSoto, TX, in 2004. Miller excelled both on the football and track and field teams (nicknamed the Eagles). Miller made 37 tackles in his junior year for the Eagles and more than doubled that number in his senior **campaign**, making 76 tackles to go with 6 quarterback sacks. He was ranked 15th in the nation among outside defensive ends.

Miller received offers to play college football at several schools, including:

- University of Florida
- University of Oklahoma
- University of Mississippi
- Texas Tech University
- Texas A&M University

Miller visited Mississippi and Texas A&M in January 2007 even though he had decided to commit to A&M in October of 2006 to become an Aggie (Texas A&M's nickname).

VON MILLER, SUPERSTAR IN THE MAKING

Video highlights sent to college recruiters demonstrated just how talented DeSoto High School's number 40, Von Miller, was at playing the positions of both defensive end and linebacker. Watching the video, you can see just how difficult Miller was for offensive lineman to handle as he consistently finds his way straight to the quarterback for the sack.

The beginning of the road for Von Miller, as seen in these video highlights from his senior year at DeSoto High School, DeSoto, TX, in 2007.

COLLEGE

Miller began playing for the Texas A&M University Aggies football team in the fall of 2007. He played in a total of 47 games over four seasons for the Aggies. His best season was his junior year, where he made 47 tackles, nearly half (21.5) for a loss in yardage, 17 sacks, and 4 fumbles.

Miller played college football for the Aggies of Texas A&M University in College Station, TX.

After Miller's freshman season in 2007, he was named to *The Sporting News* Freshman All-Big 12 team. A coaching change in his sophomore year brought former Green Bay Packers coach Mike Sherman to College Station (TX), and resulted in a change in Miller's position from defensive end to a cross between a DE and linebacker. This allowed Miller to better utilize his speed, size, and situational awareness on the field, resulting in an increase in tackles, sacks, and fumbles he was involved in or created.

Miller was named to the All-Big 12 team in 2009 at the end of his junior season, in which he posted his highest sack total of 17. His sack total in 2009 led both the Big 12 and the NCAA and his 33 sacks for his career are the best ever in the Big 12 and ranked 6th for career sacks in the NCAA.

The Aggies play at the 100,000-capacity Kyle Field.

HOME OF THE 12TH MAN

These are his career numbers at A&M:

Year	Position	Games	Tackles	Sacks	INT	Forced Fumbles
2007 (FR)	DE	9	22	2.0	0	1
2008 (SO)	DE	12	44	3.5	0	2
2009 (JR)	DE	13	47	17.0	0	4
2010 (SR)	LB	13	68	10.5	1	0
Totals		47	181	33.0	1	7

At the end of the 2010 season, Miller was honored with All-American recognition and poised to be considered highly in the 2011 NFL Draft.

VON MILLER
DRAFT DAY

Von Miller was the 2nd overall selection in the draft, chosen by the Denver Broncos.

NFL DRAFT DAY 2011
SIGNIFICANT ACTIONS

- The 2011 NFL Draft was held at Radio City Music Hall in New York City on April 28–30, 2011.

- Cam Newton, the 2010 Heisman Trophy winner from Auburn University was the 1st overall draft selection, picked by the Carolina Panthers.

- Miller was the first linebacker drafted in the 2011 NFL Draft.

- Miller was one of forty linebackers taken in the 2011 NFL Draft.

- Of the forty linebackers selected, only eleven are still active in the NFL (2017).

- Cheta Ozougwu, defensive end from Rice University (located in Houston, TX), was the last player drafted (named "Mr. Irrelevant") in the 7th round by the Houston Texans.

- The top three positions selected in the draft were Cornerbacks (thirty-nine), Linebackers (thirty-two), and Wide Receivers (twenty-eight).

- The bottom three positions drafted were Fullbacks (six), Punters (one), and, Kickers (one).

- Washington had the most selections (twelve) in the 2011 draft.

- Four teams had the fewest selections (five) in the 2011 draft: Chicago Bears, Detroit Lions, Indianapolis Colts, and Jacksonville Jaguars.

NFL DRAFT DAY 2011

Coming into the 2011 draft, Miller measured up as follows for the NFL scouts at the NFL Combine held in Indianapolis, IN:

- Measurements (height, weights): 6 feet 2.625 inches (1.9 m), 246 lbs (112 kg)
- 40-yard dash: 4.53 seconds
- 3-cone: 6.7 seconds
- Vertical jump: 37 inches (0.94 m)
- Broad jump: 10 feet 6 inches (3.20 m)

The scouts at the combine gave him a draft grade of 8.68, which rated him as a potential perennial all-pro. The overall opinion of Miller as a pro, as given by the scouts, was:

"Miller was the Butkus Award winner as the nation's top linebacker, and it seems like his game will translate very well to the next level. He is a great athlete that has prototypical size and very good instincts for the linebacker position. He is at his best as a pass rusher in a 3-4 defense, as he is explosive and strong with an arsenal of pass rushing moves. He may lack the size to consistently anchor against the run, but he flashes the ability to disengage from blockers and is an underrated run stopper. Overall, Miller is an excellent prospect that could get drafted in the top 10.

"STRENGTHS Miller has prototypical size and can flat out run. Explosive first step and closing burst makes him a terror as an edge rusher. Reads quickly, fills fast and delivers violent shots in the running game. Sound tackler that breaks down the ball carrier in the open field and consistently wraps. Hard working kid that shows a relentless motor.

"WEAKNESSES Does not have a thick lower half and at times will struggle to disengage from bigger offensive tackles in the running game. Takes poor angles at times in run support. Lacks the experience in man coverage and will not be able to cover more athletic tight ends."

MILLER VERSUS 2011 NFL LINEBACKER DRAFT CLASS

A total of forty linebackers (including Miller) were selected in the first seven rounds of the 2011 NFL Draft. Here is a summary of the top five linebackers selected (in the 1st and 2nd rounds of the draft) with Von Miller:

- **Aldon Smith,** University of Missouri (drafted by the San Francisco 49ers, 1st round, 7th selection overall) – Smith was taken by the 49ers five picks after Miller. Smith was highly regarded as a 4-3 or 3-4 defense linebacker and compared to Miller's teammate, nine-time Pro Bowler and seven-time All-Pro DeMarcus Ware. After a Pro Bowl season in 2012, Smith was cut by the Niners in 2014 and picked up by the Raiders, where he played nine games until he was suspended by the league for personal conduct issues in 2015.

- **Ryan Kerrigan,** Purdue University (drafted by Washington, 1st round, 16th selection overall) – Kerrigan was an All-American at Purdue. After his first pro year, Kerrigan was selected to the league's All-Rookie team and has since played in three Pro Bowls (2012, 2016, 2017) for Washington.

- **Akeem Ayers,** UCLA (drafted by the Tennessee Titans, 2nd round, 39th selection overall) – Ayers played a total of 91 games between 2011–2016 for Tennessee, New England, St. Louis, Indianapolis, and the New York Giants. Ayers, who won a Super Bowl with the Patriots in 2014, has 218 tackles and 15.5 sacks in his career through 2017.

- **Bruce Carter,** University of North Carolina (drafted by the Dallas Cowboys, 2nd round, 40th selection overall) – Bruce Carter is a former high school quarterback and running back who rushed for over a thousand yards in his senior year. He has played in 90 games through 2017, 36 of them as a starter, and is a member of the New York Jets with 217 career tackles and 5 sacks.

Ryan Kerrigan was the 16th pick of the draft and became a three-time Pro Bowler for Washington.

- **Brooks Reed,** University of Arizona (drafted by the Houston Texans, 2nd round, 42nd selection overall) – Reed, who is currently a member of the Atlanta Falcons, has 164 tackles, 20.5 sacks, 3 forced fumbles, and an interception in his career through 2017. He has switched from the linebacker position to defensive end for the Falcons.

Here are the important statistics of these linebackers drafted in 2011:

Player	Round, Pick	Games	Tackles	Sacks	INT	Fumbles	Pro Bowl	All-Pro	Super Bowl
Aldon Smith	1, 7	59	141	47.5	1	6	1	1	0
Ryan Kerrigan*	1, 16	102	250	62.5	3	20	2	0	0
Akeem Ayers	2, 39	91	218	15.5	4	4	0	0	1
Bruce Carter*	2, 40	82	217	5.0	5	0	0	0	0
Brooks Reed*	2, 42	94	154	19.5	1	3	0	0	0

* still active in the league

RESEARCH PROJECT:

It is rare to see many top picks in the NFL play an entire four years of college football, particularly in a top-level conference or program like the Big 12 or Texas A&M University. Fear of injury or having a bad final season can be the difference between being drafted in the 1st round or the 7th round at a cost of millions of dollars. Not only did Von Miller play his entire four years at Texas A&M, he was selected 2nd overall in the 2011 NFL Draft (he also graduated on time with a degree in poultry science). In the past ten NFL drafts, beginning in 2008, what percentage of the top ten players taken in each draft accomplished the following:

- Played all four years of college football (percentage and player's name/ school attended).
- Graduated with a degree before being drafted (percentage and player's name/ school attended).

TEXT-DEPENDENT QUESTIONS:

1. Of the six linebackers selected in the first two rounds of the 2011 NFL Draft (including Von Miller), how many are still active in the league as of the 2017 season?
2. How many linebackers in total were drafted in the 2011 NFL Draft?
3. Which team(s) had the most draft selections in the 2011 NFL Draft? Which team(s) had the fewest draft selections in the 2011 NFL Draft?

WORDS TO UNDERSTAND

POULTRY – domesticated birds kept for eggs or meat

SUBSTANCE ABUSE – the misuse or overuse of drugs, including prescription (those prescribed by a physician) and illegal drugs, and alcohol

VIOLATING – doing something that is not allowed by (a law, rule, etc.)

CHAPTER 3

ON THE FIELD

CAREER COMPARISONS

Von Miller's career has been on the rise, especially after a 2013 that included a six-game suspension for Miller at the beginning of the season for **violating** the league's **substance abuse** policy and a season ending injury that kept him from playing in Super Bowl XLVIII.

Here's how Miller's career looks when compared to some of the great linebackers of all-time:

- **Dick Butkus** (Chicago Bears, 1965–1973) – Perhaps considered the gold standard of linebackers, Butkus played his entire nine-year career with the Chicago Bears. He appeared in eight Pro Bowl games in his career and was named an All-Pro five times. The quality and level of his play resulted in his being inducted in Pro Football's Hall of Fame in Canton, OH, in 1979.

Hall of Fame Chicago Bears legend Dick Butkus is considered to be the gold standard at the linebacker position.

- **Ray Nitschke** (Green Bay Packers, 1958–1972) – Before there was Dick Butkus, there was Ray Nitschke. The legendary Green Bay Packers linebacker, who made 25 INTs in his fifteen-year NFL career, was an identifiable component of the Packers dominance in the 1960s as they were winners of five NFL championships (1961, 1962, 1965–1967) and the first two NFL Super Bowls. Nitschke was named MVP of the 1962 NFL Championship game and compiled 15 tackles and a sack in his two Super Bowl appearances.

- **Ray Lewis** (Baltimore Ravens, 1996–2012) – How good was Ray Lewis at the linebacker position? 41.5 sacks, 31 INTs, 17 forced fumbles and (like Von Miller) a Super Bowl MVP (SB XXXV in 2000) say he was exceptional. The two-time Super Bowl Champion made thirteen Pro Bowls including ten All-Pros (seven as a first teamer). Lewis was named AP Defensive Player of the Year twice. His 1,562 career tackles put him just behind former Atlanta Falcons LB Jessie Tuggle and ahead of Cleveland Brown great Clay Matthews, Jr. as the best tacklers in NFL history.

- **Lawrence Taylor** (New York Giants, 1981–1993) – Taylor is often considered the greatest if not one of the greatest players in NFL history. Taylor's play and style defined the linebacker position in the 1980s. The 2nd overall pick in the 1981 NFL Draft (the same draft position as Miller), Taylor appeared in ten Pro Bowls, all on the first-team, in his thirteen-year NFL career. He played in two winning Super Bowls, was the winner of the Bert Bell Award, and a three-time AP Defensive Player of the Year. Taylor is one of the few defensive players to also be named the league's overall MVP. Taylor became a member of the Hall of Fame in 1999.

- **Derrick Thomas** (Kansas City Chiefs, 1989–1999) – For his career, Derrick Thomas made 126.5 sacks, and became a Pro Football Hall of Fame inductee in 2009. He was the defensive leader of the Kansas City Chiefs and his hard-hitting style and unwavering focus on sacking the quarterback and disrupting the offensive backfield, makes him one of the few players Von Miller is often compared with.

VON MILLER

DENVER BRONCOS

LINEBACKER

VON MILLER

Date of birth: March 26, 1989
Height: 6 feet, 3 inches (1.91 m), Weight: Approx. 250 lbs (113 kg)
Drafted in the 1st round in 2011 (2nd pick overall) by the Denver Broncos
College: Texas A&M University

CAREER

GAMES	SACKS	TACKLES	INTS	FF
104	83.5	324	1	22

- MVP, Super Bowl (2016)

- AP Defensive Rookie of the Year (2011)

- Two-time Butkus Award Winner, College (2010) and NFL (2012)

- Appeared in six Pro Bowls (2011, 2012, 2014, 2015, 2016, 2017)

- Named First-Team All-Pro three times (2014, 2015, 2016)

- Holds the single season sack record for the Denver Broncos with 18.5 (2012)

- Selected as First-Team All-American (2009, 2010)

- Selected as First-Team All-Big 12 Conference (2009, 2010)

- Played high school football at DeSoto High School (DeSoto, TX), 2004–2007

LINEBACKER

Statistics for quarterback sacks and tackles were not maintained on a regular basis until the 1980s; information about how good players like Butkus, Nitschke, and other NFL players of the past were in the sack department is non-existent. Lawrence Taylor was credited with 132.5 sacks for his thirteen-year career with the New York Giants; Derrick Thomas made 126.5 sacks as an eleven-year member of the Kansas City Chiefs while Ray Lewis of the Baltimore Ravens is the only player in NFL history credited with at least 40 sacks (41.5) and 30 interceptions (31).

Comparing Von Miller's sack totals to the greatest sack leaders in NFL history at similar points in their careers finds that his numbers put him on pace to possibly become the all-time leader in the category:

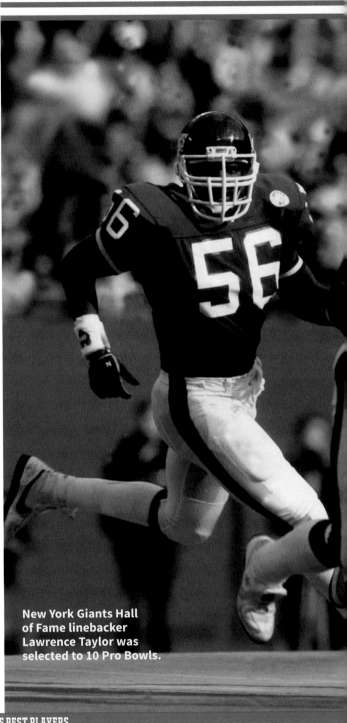

New York Giants Hall of Fame linebacker Lawrence Taylor was selected to 10 Pro Bowls.

OVERCOMING ADVERSITY

The 2013 NFL season admittedly was not one of the best seasons for Von Miller. After being named the NFL Defensive Rookie of the Year in 2011 and Butkus Award winner in 2012, he was suspended at the beginning of the 2013 season for violating the league's substance abuse policy. After serving a six-game suspension, Miller tore his ACL in game against the Houston Texans on December 22, 2013, ending his season. He bounced back in 2014 to finish with 14 sacks and help position the Broncos for a Super Bowl run the following season.

Video, showing Von Miller's season-ending ACL injury in 2013, which caused him to miss playing in Super Bowl XLVIII for the Broncos.

Player	Years	Seasons	Sacks	Tackles	Int	Forced Fumbles	NFL Sack Leader
Reggie White	1985–1990	6	94.0	530	0	9	1987, 1988
Bruce Smith	1985–1991	7	78.0	434	0	13	NA
Chris Doleman	1985–1990	6	52.5	371	3	15	1989
Jason Taylor	1997–2002	7	52.5	172	3	11	2002
Michael Strahan	1993–1999	7	47.0	234	3	9	NA
Von Miller	2011–2017	7	83.5	324	1	22	NA

Comparing the same number of years, Miller ranks just below 2006 Hall of Fame inductee Reggie White, 2nd all-time in the NFL for career sacks at 198 (White played his first season in the USFL for the Memphis Showboats, where he recorded 23.5 sacks). At his current pace, Miller may very well surpass White and all-time NFL sack leader Bruce Smith (202 career sacks).

VON MILLER VERSUS J.J. WATT

How good is Von Miller, the 2nd overall pick in the 2011 draft, versus J.J. Watt, the 11th overall pick in the draft? Pound for pound, Miller and Watt are two of the best in the game, playing outside **linebacker** and defensive end respectively. Their paths to the NFL could not have been any further apart coming out of high school. Miller was one of the top rated outside **linebackers** in the country being recruited out of high school. Watt was initially a tight end that received little attention coming from Pewaukee High School in Pewaukee, WI.

Miller played four years at Texas A&M University, graduating with a bachelor's degree in **poultry** science. Watt played a year at Central Michigan University as a TE before transferring to the University of Wisconsin and switching positions to defensive

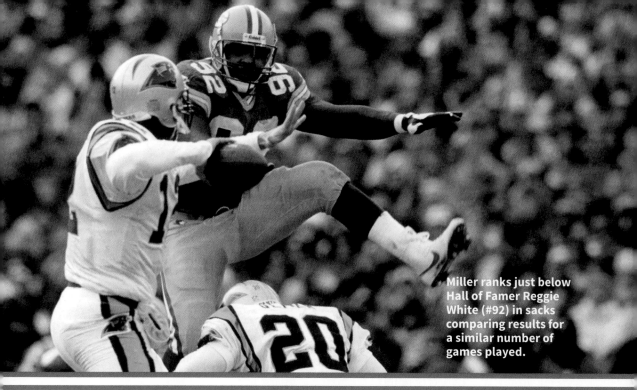

Miller ranks just below Hall of Famer Reggie White (#92) in sacks comparing results for a similar number of games played.

end. Both became All-Americans and received high marks by pro scouts and have been outstanding professional players at this point in their careers.

Here are the career numbers for both Von Miler and J.J. Watt through 2017:

Player	Round, Pick	Games	Tackles	Sacks	INT	Forced Fumbles	Pro Bowl	All-Pro	Super Bowl
Von Miller	1, 2	104	324	83.5	1	22	6	3	1
J.J. Watt	1, 11	88	310	76.0	1	15	4	4	0

Comparing the two shows that both superstar athletes have collected quite a bit of hardware (i.e. trophies, awards) between the two of them. It is no doubt that Watt and Miller are a good as it gets in terms of defensive players in the NFL today. Here is a short list of some of the awards both players have racked up in their respective NFL careers:

Two of the best in the league on the field, Miller (third from R) and J.J. Watt (second from R) work together off the field as well, seen here on a 2013 USO Tour in Kandahar, Afghanistan.

- Super Bowl MVP (Miller: 2016)

- NFL AP Defensive Player of the Year (Watt, three times: 2012, 2014, 2015)

- NFL Bert Bell Award Winner (Watt: 2014)

- NFL Butkus Award Winner (Miller: 2012)

- NFL Pro Bowl (Miller, six times: 2011–2012, 2014–2017; Watt, four times: 2012–2015)

- NFL First-Team All-Pro (Miller, three times: 2012, 2015–2016; Watt, four times: 2012–2015)

- NFL Top 100 (Miller, six times: 2012–2017; Watt, five times: 2013–2017)

With all of the recognition and awards between Von Miller and J.J. Watt, it would only be fitting to see both of these great players enter Pro Football's Hall of Fame in Canton, OH, at the same time, side by side.

VON MILLER
IN THE PLAYOFFS

Von Miller has appeared in the playoffs seven times, including a wild card game, four divisional round games, one AFC Championship game and one Super Bowl appearance (Miller was injured toward the end of the 2013 season and missed playing Super Bowl XLVIII). Here is how he has performed in the playoffs:

Date	Opponent	W/L	DenSC	OppSC	Tackles	Sacks	INT	Fumbles
1/8/2012	Pittsburgh	W	29	23	3	1.0	0	0
1/14/2012	New England	L	10	45	0	0.0	0	0
1/12/2013	Baltimore	L	35	38	7	0.5	0	0
1/11/2015	Indianapolis	L	13	24	5	0.0	0	0
1/17/2016	Pittsburgh	W	23	16	2	0.0	0	0
1/24/2016	New England	W	20	18	4	2.5	1	0
2/7/2016	Carolina	W	24	10	5	2.5	0	2
			TOTAL		26	6.5	1	2
			AVG PER GAME		3.71	0.93	0.14	0.29

Miller's best playoff stretch came in 2016, when he faced QBs Ben Roethlisberger (Pittsburgh Steelers), Tom Brady (New England Patriots), and Cam Newton (Carolina Panthers), who had been named the NFL's AP Offensive Player of the Year and Bert Bell Player of the Year for the 2015 season. Newton, who was drafted just ahead of Miller as the 1st overall pick in 2011, was the AP Offensive Rookie of the Year opposite Miller's defensive award.

Miller recorded a total of 11 tackles, 5 sacks (2.5 each against Brady and Newton), an interception (against Brady), and 2 forced fumbles, one that was recovered for a

In Super Bowl 50, Miller and the Broncos faced the Carolina Panthers, led by Cam Newton, who was drafted one spot ahead of Miller in the 2011 NFL Draft.

touchdown in Super Bowl 50. His Super Bowl performance alone has been described as the best defensive performance in this type of game since former Baltimore Ravens Ray Lewis won the MVP award for his performance in Super Bowl XXXV (2001).

RESEARCH PROJECT:

Von Miller is one of the few players to be named the most outstanding linebacker in the country in both college and the pros. He was recognized in 2010 and again in 2012 as the winner of the Butkus Award, giving to the best linebacker in the country at the high school, college, and NFL levels. The award is named after the legendary former Chicago Bears great linebacker and Hall of Famer Dick Butkus. Here's an easy research project: identify and list the players who have won the Butkus Award in both college and the NFL. Then find the players who have won the Butkus Award in high school and college; if these players are in the NFL, compare their career numbers to Miller's.

TEXT-DEPENDENT QUESTIONS:

1. Which defensive award did Miller win in 2011?
2. How many total quarterback sacks has Von Miller made in the playoffs? How many total tackles have been credited to Miller in the playoffs?
3. How many times has Von Miller been named a First-Team NFL All-Pro?

WORDS TO UNDERSTAND

DEBILITATING – to make (someone or something) weak

PROTEST – the act of objecting or a gesture of disapproval

SOLIDARITY – a feeling of unity between people who have the same interests or goals

SPECIAL TEAMS – a unit of the football team that handles the punting and kicking duties, including kickoffs, extra point attempts, and field goals

CHAPTER 4

WORDS COUNT

When the time comes to address the media before or after a game, players either retreat to the comfort of traditional phrases that avoid controversy (Cliché City), or they speak their mind with refreshing candor (Quote Machine).

Here are ten quotes from Von Miller, compiled in part from the website BrainyQuotes. com (with additional quotes from the Reuters newswire), with some context provided as to the meaning of what he is talking about or referencing.

Miller's signature look revolves around his collection of black-rimmed glasses, which he wears more than his substantial shoe collection.

"I'm at my best when people are depending on me. If it's just on me and I don't have nothing to do, I'm going to be lazy. On the football field, it's every single day, every play, knowing that people are depending on me to make my play. That helps me elevate my game to another level."

Miller excels when the pressure is on and others depend on him to raise his level of play. When on the football field, his desire to compete rises, raising him to a higher performance level. **Rating: Quote Machine**

"I really don't look at myself as a defensive end or a linebacker or a cornerback or a safety. I don't try to limit myself to just rushing the passer or dropping back in coverage or being a run-stopper; I try to be great at football."

Since his debut in the NFL in 2011, Miller has worked to establish himself as the one of the top, if not the best linebacker in the game. Miller however sees himself as a complete defender, able to compete wherever he plays. **Rating: Quote Machine**

"The crazy thing is I got all of these shoes, and probably 80 percent of them I've never worn before. I've worn all the glasses. I sleep in them, bend them up a little bit. Glasses are on all the time except when I'm at practice or at work."

Von Miller has two passions beyond football: glasses and shoes. Glasses are truly what define Von Miller's style and are a big part of his community involvement, as he has created a foundation around providing glasses to low-income children in Denver. **Rating: Quote Machine**

"I like the sci-fi channel. Just science in general. I came across a segment on time travel and how time travel is possible. We create a spaceship that's moving at almost the speed of light, we go in that spaceship in outer space, and we fly around for a year, when we get back to Earth, Earth would've aged 10 years."

Miller is certainly celebrated for his quirky, off-the-cuff sayings and mannerisms in the locker room, on the field, and in life in general. While the accuracy of the information he recalls in the quote is in question, Miller's love of science and his general thirst for knowledge are no work of fiction. **Rating: Quote Machine**

Time travel through outer space is one of the many science fiction theories that Miller ponders.

This quote came after Miller signed a six-year, $115 million contract on July 15, 2016, with $70 million in guaranteed money. Although the Broncos labeled him a franchise player in order to keep him from going to another team, Miller's new contract made him the highest-paid defensive player in NFL history (and the guaranteed portion is the most ever paid to a defensive player). Miller expressed his feelings over being able to call himself a Bronco for at least six more years by saying the things all players say when they sign a new deal. **Rating: Cliché City**

"I'm super happy and excited to be back with my teammates for the next six years. This is something I really wanted—to stay with the Denver Broncos, I'm excited for the future and ready to get back to work."

"All these guys helped to get me here, back to back, right?"

The Denver Broncos were completely destroyed by the Seattle Seahawks in Super Bowl XLVIII by the score of 43–8 on February 2, 2014. Miller missed the game due to injury, but it was not his last chance to perform on football's biggest stage. Perseverance and hard work paid off as Denver ended up winning the AFC Championship on January 24, 2016, (20–18) for the opportunity to play in Super Bowl 50. Although not quite back to back as Miller states in the quote, the Broncos redeemed their earlier loss to Seattle with a 24–10 victory. Miller's efforts in the game, with the support of his teammates, allowed him to become MVP of the game. For the fact that Miller completely ignores the entire 2014 season this gets an original rating. **Rating: Quote Machine**

Miller reluctantly admits that he believes New England quarterback Tom Brady is the greatest of all time.

"I mean, Brady's the GOAT [Greatest of All-Time], but I feel like Peyton Manning is the real GOAT. I'm going to go with my guy. I'm going to go with Peyton. But, I mean, Tom Brady is the GOAT. Brady's playing until 40, and he looks like he can play until he's 45. Some other guys, they can't make it that many years. It's all different. That all falls into the equation of Tom Brady being the GOAT."

This is a quote of MIler's that was made just prior to a Sunday Night Football between the Denver Broncos and New England Patriots on November 12, 2017. Miller starts by calling Patriot QB Brady the greatest, then quickly says his QB Manning is the real greatest, before anointing Brady the greatest once again, and then concluding that it all points to Brady after all. Classic **Rating: Quote Machine**

"I've had asthma my whole life. My mom used to hook the generator up to the Suburban and roll the extension cord all the way down to the football field and have my nebulizer hooked up to that so I could take treatments in between offense and defense. I was in the fifth grade when she started doing that."

Miller remarks on how a huge assist from his mother in carrying the equipment he needed to deal with his asthma when he was younger allowed him to develop as a player and overcome what is a **debilitating** condition for many young asthma sufferers. **Rating: Quote Machine**

"The Denver defense just shows the type of team we have. The Denver defense's not just about offense, defense or special teams, we came together as a whole."

Von Miller understands that for Denver to be successful, it takes a team effort that is the sum of all of its units: offense, defense, and **special teams**. The defensive unit that Miller plays on as one of its leaders and stars is only effective when the other parts of the team are good and performing at their maximum potential. This quote is muddled at best, but there's a cliché in there trying hard to get out. **Rating: Cliché City**

Von Miller comments on how he bulked up from just around 200 pounds when he was a high school player in DeSoto, TX, to nearly 272 pounds in his third year in the NFL (a near twenty-five percent gain in weight). He speculates whether the additional pounds gained contributed to the injury which limited him to only nine games played in 2013 and convinced him to make the changes necessary to bring his weight down. He weighed 237 pounds for the 2017 season, down 35 lbs from his heaviest weight. **Rating: Quote Machine**

> **"Out of high school, I was, like, 202–205 pounds. My rookie season, I was, like, 245; my second year, I was 255. My third year, I got up to like 272, and I tore my ACL. I don't know if my weight was part of the cause of that, but I got hurt, so I just tried to re-evaluate my situation."**

VON MILLER AND 2017 RACIAL INJUSTICE PROTESTS

The beginning of the 2017 NFL season was one of controversy around the league as players exercised their First Amendment right to **protest** racial injustice prior to the start of their games. At issue was an approach by players throughout the league to be in **solidarity** with one another over the issue of equal treatment by the police of members of minority communities.

Prior to the start of several games, players locked arms and knelt during the singing of the National Anthem, to protest recent high-profile cases of deadly misconduct against minority citizens by law enforcement officers. Some groups, including the president of the United States and his administration, tried to diminish the protests by complaining

they were disrespectful to those that had served in the military under the American flag.

Thirty-two Denver Broncos players, including Von Miller, took a knee as part of the league-wide players protest before the start of a September 24, 2017, game against the Buffalo Bills, which the Broncos lost 26–16. Miller explained the action taken by the two teams:

> "Me and my teammates, we felt like [the President]'s speech was an assault on our most cherished right, freedom of speech, and collectively, we felt like we had to do something for this game. If not any other game—not in the past, not in the future—at this moment in time, we felt like as a team that we had to do something. We couldn't just let things go.

COACH, I'M DELICATE!

Von Miller has taken his place in line as the latest pitchman for Old Spice deodorant. In one of the funnier ads of 2017, Miller's fictitious coach finds out that Miller has a delicate side.

Miller displaying his acting chops in this fun Old Spice commercial.

"I have a huge respect for the military and our protective services. I've been to Afghanistan. I've met real-life superheroes. It wasn't any disrespect to them. It was for my brothers that had been attacked for things that they do during the game. I felt like I had to join them.

"I felt like it was an attack on the National Football League as well. You know, he went on and talked about ratings. This is my life, and I love everything about the National Football League. . . . I try to keep out any politics or social issues and just try to play ball. But I feel like it was an attack on us."

RESEARCH PROJECT:

Von Miller suffered from asthma as a child. Find another example of a player in NFL history who overcame a serious childhood disease and was able to become a celebrated player and award winner at the professional football level. Describe:

- the player's name (position played, years, team, awards, Hall of Fame)
- the disease
- how it affected the player's life early on
- what was done to overcome the disease

TEXT-DEPENDENT QUESTIONS:

1. What do the initials G.O.A.T. stand for? Which two players were Von Miller referring to as being GOATs?
2. How many players including Miller decided to take a knee as a symbol of protest before the start of a September 24, 2017, NFL game?
3. For which game was Miller named MVP?

WORDS TO UNDERSTAND

CONSUMMATE – extremely skilled and accomplished

CORRECTIVE – intended to make something better

COOP – a cage or small enclosure (as for poultry)

STIGMA – a mark of shame or discredit

CHAPTER 5

OFF THE FIELD

CHICKEN FARMING ISN'T EASY

Von Miller graduated from Texas A&M University with an unusual degree. It was not in business or communications, but rather in poultry farming. That's right, one of the most feared linebackers in the game is a chicken farmer in Texas during the offseason.

Miller, in an interview with *ESPN The Magazine*, spoke about the small tennis court sized **coop** full of chickens that he maintains in his hometown of DeSoto, TX, where his parents live (and where he grew up playing football). The idea of becoming a chicken

Miller's college degree is in poultry farming.

A SPECIAL BOND

Von Miller is all business when on the football field, motivating his teammates through his words and actions. He is definitely far more loose and jovial away from the gridiron, whether it's at home raising his chickens or doing commercials that feature his humor and dance moves. One of the things that has kept him grounded however through all of his trials and tribulations, like his six-game suspension and ACL injury in 2013, is his mother Gloria. Miller talks about his relationship with his mother in this NFL Films feature.

GLORIA MILLER
VON'S MOM

VON MILLER
BRONCOS LINEBACKER

Von Miller opens up to NFL Films to discuss the special bond between him and his mother Gloria Miller.

farmer began as a way to earn an easy grade while he attended A&M as a student-athlete but grew into a passion for him.

Miller Farm, as he has come to call his spread, specializes in humanely raised, grass-fed chickens that produce fresh, USDA Grade A eggs. Miller takes pride in being able to provide plenty of space for his birds to roam and live long, productive lives laying eggs for his consumption and eventually to become a part of a larger commercial operation that he would like to purchase as he heads toward retirement.

ANOTHER DANCING STAR

Almost every season finds some present or past NFL player trying their hand (or feet) on the dance floor in the celebrity dance competition, *Dancing with the Stars*. In 2016, Miller became the latest player to be asked to perform on the show, appearing in Season 22 with his partner, professional dancer Witney Carson. Miller's appearance on *Dancing with the Stars* puts him in the company of the following current and former players:

- Donald Driver (former) – Green Bay
- Jerry Rice (former) – San Francisco/Oakland and Hall of Fame inductee
- Antonio Brown – Pittsburgh
- Emmett Smith (former) – Dallas and Hall of Fame inductee
- Kurt Warner (former) – St. Louis/Arizona and Hall of Fame inductee
- Lawrence Taylor (former) – New York Giants and Hall of Fame inductee
- Jason Taylor (former) – Miami/Washington and Hall of Fame inductee
- Chad "Ochocinco" Johnson (former) – Cincinnati and other teams
- Calvin "Megatron" Johnson Jr. (former) – Detroit
- Hines Ward (former) – Pittsburgh

Miller competed in the 2016 season of TV talent contest *Dancing with the Stars*.

- Warren Sapp (former) – Tampa Bay/Oakland and Hall of Fame inductee
- Michael Irvin (former) – Dallas Cowboys and Hall of Fame inductee
- Rashad Jennings – NY Giants
- Doug Flutie (former) – Buffalo and other teams
- Jacoby Jones – Baltimore

Miller gave his best effort during the competition but succumbed during a double-elimination episode in May 2016, finishing eighth in the competition.

GIVING BACK TO THE COMMUNITY

VON'S VISION/BACK TO SCHOOL VISION DAY

In addition to suffering from asthma, Miller also had poor vision as a child, requiring him to wear glasses. The thick-rimmed black glasses that he wears today are part of his signature look. Having glasses has been a source of pride for Miller in that he was raised in a family fortunate enough to have the means to identify his vision problem early on and afford the necessary eyewear to correct his vision.

Von's Vision fairs provides free eye exams to children in need, and if vision problems are detected, glasses are also ordered for them at no cost.

Beginning in 2015, Miller began hosting Von's Vision fairs for low-income students in Denver. The purpose of the fairs is to provide eye examinations at no cost to help determine if a child is in need of glasses. If a need for **corrective** lenses is identified, Miller, in partnership with several national eyewear and vision screening companies, has glasses ordered and presents each child with new glasses, free of charge, during a party.

The vision days serve many purposes. They allow Miller, the **consummate** child at heart, an opportunity to interact with the children and remove any **stigma** associated with wearing glasses. Several hundred school-aged children in Denver have benefitted from Von Miller's generosity and thoughtfulness. He has taken time at each of the vision day events to spend time with the children, sporting his own glasses, to show that wearing glasses can be cool and not something to be ashamed about. After all, who is going to say anything otherwise to an NFL linebacker who is also a Super Bowl champion and MVP?

MARKETING VON MILLER

Miller joins a list of Old Spice pitchmen including former Green Bay Packer and Minnesota Vikings WR Greg Jennings, actor/comedian Terry Crews (who played linebacker/defensive end briefly for the Los Angeles Rams, San Diego, and Washington) and probably the

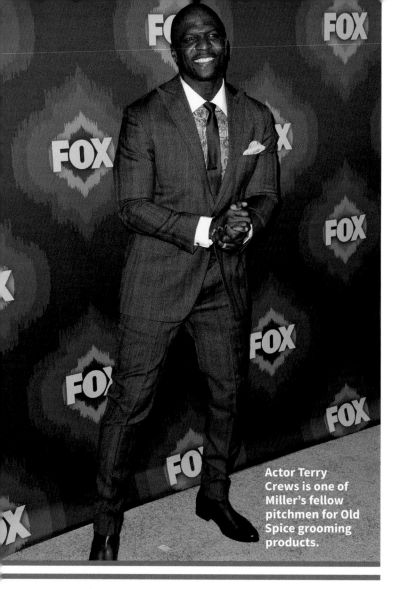

Actor Terry Crews is one of Miller's fellow pitchmen for Old Spice grooming products.

most recognizable of the group, Isaiah Mustafa, a former practice squad member of the Tennessee Titans, Cleveland Browns, Oakland Raiders, and Seattle Seahawks, who is known for the many topless ads he did for the men's care products.

Miller has been featured in several ads that have been a great showcase of his personality, humor, and range as an actor and potential comedian. He is a natural in front of the camera should he decide on a second career after pro football. In addition to ads for Old Spice, Miller has been featured in ads for the NFL, including a funny spot that appeared during Super Bowl LI. This spot features different babies who are the younger version of future NFL stars and coaches, including a mustachioed, sweater wearing Mike Ditka baby, a toddler draped in New England Patriots coach Bill Belichick's famous hoodie, and a baby wearing wide rimmed glasses and a cowboy hat that is representative of Miller and his look. The background music played is the 1984 song "You're the Inspiration," by classic rock band Chicago with the commercial's tagline reading "Born from Greatness," a fitting description of Miller and the other individuals in the ad.

Miller is also featured in an ad for EA Sports Madden NFL 17 and Xbox One S, where he plays himself, in fact, several versions of himself, singing to viewers that they should consider starting him when playing the game. The song, which is a take on pop star Justin Beiber's hit "Sorry" has Miller telling everyone that by starting him, teams will not be able to make first downs ("never going to get first downs / try and try, they won't gain no ground"). The ad also features Miller showing off some of his famous dance moves, specifically his sack dance.

Here are some of the other companies that benefit from the talents of Miller to promote and sell their products and services:

- Adidas
- Best Buy
- Chef's Cut Jerky brand
- Geek Squad
- Muzik (headphones)
- Zamst (maker of braces and compression socks)

The sense of humor that Miller brings to the small screen via advertising contrasts with the fierce competitor we enjoy watching on the field on Sundays during football season.

VON MILLER'S CONTRACT

Miller, along with his agent Joby Branion (an attorney and graduate of Duke University who founded Vanguard Sports Group) negotiated a contract extension with the Denver Broncos that was signed in July 2016. The team had previously designated Miller its "franchise player," a designation available to each NFL team to use for one contract each season to keep their best players from going to another team without having to sign them long term.

The negotiations were very successful for Miller. Not only did he and the team come to agreement on the richest contract ever offered a defensive player in NFL history ($114.5 million with $70 million in guaranteed money), he was able to remain a Denver Bronco through at least the end of 2021.

Miller has done well for himself during his career in the NFL. He has won many awards and was recognized as the most valuable player of Super Bowl 50. This honor came two seasons after Miller underwent a

Miller, a fan favorite with the Broncos, is the highest-paid defensive player in the league.

difficult 2013 season. Serving a six-game suspension and tearing his ACL that season may have been, in hindsight, a good thing. It allowed Miller to focus on what is important and set him up to become not only successful on the field but just as successful off the field.

From helping young children see and do better in school to raising chickens at his DeSoto, TX, home, Miller is shaping into an NFL superstar.

RESEARCH PROJECT:

Von Miller is not the only NFL player who wears glasses. Research and find five other players, past or present, who wore glasses while playing in the league. Provide the player's name, position, the team they played for, and the years the player was in the NFL. Of the five players, find the one who also played linebacker and played in the Super Bowl, and is now a member of the Pro Football Hall of Fame (and also what additional role he has/had in the NFL and for what team).

TEXT-DEPENDENT QUESTIONS:

1. What pop star's song did Von Miller use to convince Xbox One S players that they should start him?

2. What is the name of the annual event Von Miller holds for the benefit of Denver area school children? What is the purpose of the event?

3. What season did Von Miller appear on the dance competition Dancing with the Stars?

blitz – a defensive strategy in which one or more linebackers or defensive backs, in addition to the defensive line, attempt to overwhelm the quarterback's protection by attacking from unexpected locations or situations.

cornerbacks – the defenders primarily responsible for preventing the offenses wide receivers from catching passes, accomplished by remaining as close to the opponent as possible during pass routes. Cornerbacks are usually the fastest players on the defense.

defensive backs – a label applied to cornerbacks and safeties, or the secondary in general.

end zone – an area 10 yards deep at either end of the field bordered by the goal line and the boundaries.

field goal – an attempt to kick the ball through the uprights, worth three points. It is taken by a specialist called the place kicker. Distances are measured from the spot of the kick plus 10 yards for the depth of the end zone.

first down – the first play in a set of four downs, or when the offense succeeds in covering 10 yards in the four downs.

fumble – when a player loses possession of the ball before being tackled, normally by contact with an opponent. Either team may recover the ball. The ground cannot cause a fumble.

goal line – the line that divides the end zones from the rest of the field. A touchdown is awarded if the ball breaks the vertical plane of the goal line while in possession or if a receiver catches the ball in the end zone.

huddle – a gathering of the offense or defense to communicate the upcoming play decided by the coach.

interception – a pass caught by a defensive player instead of an offensive receiver. The ball may be returned in the other direction.

lateral – a pass or toss behind the originating player to a teammate as measured by the lines across the field. Although the offense may only make one forward pass per play, there is no limit to the number of laterals at any time.

line of scrimmage – an imaginary line, determined by the ball's location before each play, that extends across the field from sideline to sideline. Seven offensive players must be on the line of scrimmage, though the defense can set up in any formation. Forward passes cannot be thrown from beyond the line of scrimmage.

pass – when the ball is thrown to a receiver who is farther down the field. A team is limited to one such forward pass per play. Normally this is the duty of the quarterback, although technically any eligible receiver can pass the ball.

play action – a type of offensive play in which the quarterback pretends to hand the ball to a running back before passing the ball. The goal is to fool the secondary into weakening their pass coverage.

play clock – visible behind the end zone at either end of the stadium. Once a play is concluded, the offense has 40 seconds to snap the ball for the next play. The duration is reduced to 25 seconds for game-related stoppages such as penalties. Time is kept on the play clock. If the offense does not snap the ball before the play clock elapses, they incur a 5-yard penalty for delay of game.

punt – a kick, taken by a special teams player called the punter, that surrenders possession to the opposing team. This is normally done on fourth down when the offense deems gaining a first down unlikely.

receiver – an offensive player who may legally catch a pass, almost always wide receivers, tight ends, and running backs. Only the two outermost players on either end of the line of scrimmage—even wide receivers who line up distantly from the offensive line—or the four players behind the line of scrimmage (such as running backs, another wide receiver, and the quarterback) are eligible receivers. If an offensive lineman, normally an ineligible receiver, is placed on the outside of the line of scrimmage because of an unusual formation, he is considered eligible but must indicate his eligibility to game officials before the play.

run – a type of offensive play in which the quarterback, after accepting the ball from center, either keeps it and heads upfield or gives the ball to another player, who then attempts to move ahead with the help of blocking teammates.

sack – a play in which the defense tackles the quarterback behind the line of scrimmage on a pass play.

safety – 1) the most uncommon scoring play in football. When an offensive player is tackled in his own end zone, the defensive team is awarded two points and receives the ball via a kick; 2) a defensive secondary position divided into two roles, free safety and strong safety.

snap – the action that begins each play. The center must snap the ball between his legs, usually to the quarterback, who accepts the ball while immediately behind the center or several yards farther back in a formation called the shotgun.

special teams – the personnel that take the field for the punts, kickoffs, and field goals, or a generic term for that part of the game.

tackle – 1) a term for both an offensive and defensive player. The offensive tackles line up on the outside of the line, but inside the tight end, while the defensive tackles protect the interior of their line; 2) the act of forcing a ball carrier to touch the ground with any body part other than the hand or feet. This concludes a play.

tight end – an offensive player who normally lines up on the outside of either offensive tackle. Multiple tight ends are frequently employed on running plays where the offense requires only a modest gain. Roles vary between blocking or running pass routes.

touchdown – scored when the ball breaks the vertical plane of the goal line. Worth six points and the scoring team can add a single additional point by kick or two points by converting from the 2-yard line with an offensive play.

RESOURCES

FURTHER READING

Brannen, Nick. *Denver Broncos 360°*. Morrisville: Lulu Press, 2015.

Crepeau, Richard. *NFL Football: A History of America's New National Pastime*. Champaign: University of Illinois Press, 2014.

Fishman, John M. *Sports All-Stars: Von Miller*. Minneapolis: Lerner Publications, 2017.

Gitlin, Marty. *Biggest Names in Sports: Von Miller Football Star*. Lake Elmo: North Star Editions, 2017.

Leventhal, Josh. *Linebackers*. St. Paul: Black Rabbit Books, 2017.

Mason, Andrew. *Tales From the Denver Broncos Sideline: A Collection of the Greatest Broncos Stories Ever Told*. New York: Sports Publishing, 2014.

Saccomano, Jim. *The Complete Illustrated History: Denver Broncos*. Minneapolis: MBI Publishing Company, 2013.

Wilner, Barry and Ken Rappoport. *On the Clock: The Story of the NFL Draft*. Lanham: Taylor Trade Publishing, 2015.

INTERNET RESOURCES

http://bleacherreport.com/nfl

The official website for Bleacher Report Sport's NFL reports on each of the 32 teams.

https://www.cbssports.com/nfl/teams/page/DEN/denver-broncos

The web page for the Denver Broncos provided by CBSSports.com, providing latest news and information, player profiles, scheduling, and standings.

www.espn.com/

The official website of ESPN sports network.

http://www.footballdb.com/teams/nfl/denver-broncos/history

The Football Database, a reputable news source, Denver Broncos web page providing historical rosters, results, statistics, and draft information.

www.nfl.com/

The official website of the National Football League.

www.pro-football-reference.com/

The football specific resource provided by Sports Reference LLC for current and historical statistics of players, teams, scores, and leaders in the NFL, AFL, and AAFC.

http://www.denverbroncos.com/

The official website for the Denver Broncos football club, including history, player information, statistics, and news.

https://sports.yahoo.com/nfl/

The official website of Yahoo! Sports NFL coverage, providing news, statistics, and important information about the league and the 32 teams.

PHOTO CREDITS

Chapter 1
Jeffrey Beall | Wikipedia Commons
Keith Allison | Flickr

Chapter 2
Keith Allison | Flickr
© Julián Rovagnati | Dreamstime.com
© Wellesenterprises | Dreamstime.com
© Bingram | Dreamstime.com
Marianne O'Leary | Wikipedia Commons
© Theroff97 | Dreamstime.com
Ryan Kerrigan was the 16th pick of the draft and became a three-time Pro Bowler for Washington.

Chapter 3
Keith Allison | Flickr
© Jerry Coli | Dreamstime.com
© Jerry Coli | Dreamstime.com
© Jerry Coli | Dreamstime.com
Sgt. Ashley Bell | Wikipedia Commons
© Walter Arce | Dreamstime.com

Chapter 4
Trent Williams | Wikipedia Commons
Von_Miller_Trent_Williams
© Mreco99 | Dreamstime.com
© Sdecoret | Dreamstime.com
© Jenta Wong | Dreamstime.com
Keith Allison | Flickr

Chapter 5
Staff Sgt. Stephanie Rubi | Wikipedia Commons
© Neydtstock | Dreamstime.com
Serecki | Wikipedia Commons
© Darren Baker | Dreamstime.com
© Jaguarps | Dreamstime.com
Sgt. 1st Class Brian Picklesimer | Wikipedia Commons

EDUCATIONAL VIDEO LINKS

CHAPTER 1

http://x-qr.net/1DbG

http://x-qr.net/1FaS

http://x-qr.net/1Er2

http://x-qr.net/1G1H

http://x-qr.net/1Fa9

http://x-qr.net/1DVi

http://x-qr.net/1FTT

http://x-qr.net/1CrD

CHAPTER 2

http://x-qr.net/1Hji

CHAPTER 3

http://x-qr.net/1HAD

CHAPTER 4

http://x-qr.net/1GZp

CHAPTER 5

http://x-qr.net/1ErW

ABOUT THE AUTHOR

Joe L. Morgan is a father, author, and an avid sports fan. He enjoys every type of professional sport, including NFL, NBA, MLB, and European club soccer. He enjoyed a brief career as a punter and a defensive back at the NCAA Division III level, and now spends much of his time watching and writing about the sports he loves.